THE DIVERSIFICATION OF DAVE TURNIP

Paul Sutton

with illustrations by Julia Scheele

NEWTON-LE-WILLOWS

Published in the United Kingdom in 2017
by The Knives Forks And Spoons Press,
51 Pipit Avenue,
Newton-le-Willows,
Merseyside,
WA12 9RG.

ISBN 978-1-912211-00-5

Copyright © Paul Sutton, 2017.

The right of Paul Sutton to be identified as the author of this work has been asserted by him in accordance with the Copyrights, Designs and Patents Act of 1988. All rights reserved. No part of this publication may be reproduced, stored in a retrieval system, transmitted in any form or by any means, electronic, photocopying, recording or otherwise, without prior permission of the publisher.

Acknowledgements:

'The Chronicles of Dave Turnip' first appeared in a pamphlet from Original Plus and 'The Sorry History of Fast Food' in a pamphlet from Leafe Press. Some versions of other pieces have been published in Stride, Litter, The Red Ceilings Press, and International Times. Many thanks to all their editors.

Table of Contents

PROLOGUE: THE CHRONICLES OF DAVE TURNIP	7
1. A TURNIP TAKES THE VEIL	17
2. DAVE TURNIP IN HIS OWN WORDS	21
3. ANOTHER WRETCHED DAY IN BLIGHTY	35
4. THE TURNIP'S RETURN	39
5. THE SORRY HISTORY OF FAST FOOD	49
EPILOGUE (ON UVB-76)	63

PROLOGUE
THE CHRONICLES OF DAVE TURNIP

A. Turnip Adrift

Dave Turnip (poet and former punter),
enlightener of estates & concrete arterials.
The documentary films explore
some shrines in his bedroom.

The first "whore" to disappear
her mouth he can remember
engorging him, "after the
end of a relationship, finding myself
in the red-light district."

Kicks a habit and starts to chronicle.
Project born of his spunk in skinny girls,
hooded or straggling.

What is it with girls found in water,
on flooded fields and painters' light
under bridges (no Ophelia references,
I beg you cunt).

"In the feral darkness
I tasted fire and sex.
In waste-grounds and B & Q carparks,
I saw myself saviour,
Lawrence of Arabia;
to the erstwhile urchins,
I was Bilbo Baggins."

Picture any seaport in the snow,
all those pretty girls wanting to sell.
This man drives around,

meticulous about his fingernails,
has worked the construction sites
and liners, stolen from cabins
(white gold with sapphire).

Job, job, job,
up and down the sinking east coast
ports from 70s' cup replays.
Then the containers and easy pockets
filled with rye.

Dear Mr Turnip,
Your name is ridiculous.
I recall a former England boss
(came after Robson from Ipswich Town).
ACE funding for your project has no chance.
I advise contacting "Crack Down"
an outreach project
for sex workers with habits.
To find your community centre,
look for the green light.

Car on car on car,
sometimes the seagulls
sensing a change,
abandon their landfills for
outflows from factories.

Turnip as ornithologist
watches their circling
higher like snow, a helicopter can see
it pans out; the map shows geography
of movement then capture.

In old Suffolk he rests his fuddled head.
Soon he'll buy that abandoned water mill,
walk the skinny fields, crack the odd puddle.
About Dave Turnip much more shall be said.

B. Turnip in Love

To the girl with no memories, here's your past.
I found you slip-shod, hitching to Paris,
dripping on the heated leather, staring
through the droplets at a new-found country.

How much fat will there be to protect me?
Fallen economically, we're finished;
I am corrupted and my core has gone.
Don't count on decency, brains scream at night.

Bus stop indignities, you all alone,
moron mutterings praised and paid in full.
The good feelings caused this, the left to blame,
stamping, eating to shit successfully.

C. Turnip on Manoeuvres

Dave Turnip is the "local poet helping
Suffolk police pursue their enquiries."

Studies the street girls carnally – and has
washed their hair. It takes seven hours as

the heroin meanders slowly through them.
He waits up, does the new paperwork then

offers each a restorative fry-up,
or lifts to any car-park they fancy.

Even in a light-infested city,
dead zones made of darkness.

A pedestrian wanders through.
A camera tracks the movement –

their coupling seen through his
reflex spasm – over in a moment.

D. The Haunting of Dave Turnip

DT uses now just his initials.
Having read *A Glastonbury Romance*
Turnip speeds over Somerset's levels,
to a room pre-booked in a pricey pub.

Turnip adrift, wanderer
over half-built estates and
slip roads unlit in moonlight.
Brings degree certificates
to show qualifications:
MBA; PGCE;
oh how the world has tilted.

Glastonbury for its ghosts.
Arriving under lake light,
pale prince on a dripping bus.
One road, and off it this inn,
narrow stairs behind the bar,
epilepsy carpet, through
fire doors to a lonely bulb.

Such weight, pressed for confession;
(prison yard pictures of men
without pleas). So now Turnip
cannot rise, squeaks in surprise,
a hooded man comes calling
for skinheads and patriots,
sitting on his skinny chest.

Witnessing disinterment,
feverish notes to himself
scrawled under swinging lamplight.
Joins a guild of gravediggers;
"no bugger is interested"
snaps some attempted pickup.

Turnip needs more property.
Wherefrom (you say) comes his cash?
Several redundancies,
share-saves and annuities:
a ditch-encircled cottage,
still the waters lap at him,
late driver (headlights undipped)
spots our drunkard moonraking.

Abandoning syllabics;
bored with the seven counting,
headshakes, like birds pulling worms,
embarrassing simile.
Decides on prose poetry,
reads Céline, distilling rage,
attempting his ellipsis.

"All my life, form and counting ... oh to abandon it ... I met him by chance ... how travel once bored me ... I lost my books in Munich ... re-read Le Carré and Christie ... one Sunday ... we hugged like survivors and swapped bags ... I carried his to the pension ... extra rooms? no problem ... someone on the run ...attracting departing shoulders ... checks corners ... the empty stillness of the sloping sea ... a coast for concealment ... Looking outwards ... he said nothing."

So began the haunting of Dave Turnip.

E. Turnip Resurgam

In the Central African Republic
where his name means nothing,
melting in the heat and mud,
tramping on absurdly through.

Astounded by the mountains in mist,
everything slithering, khaki villages,
soaked and sky-lowering, in warm rain
he suspects unspeakable acts.

A period in France, researching his hero,
befriended by bitter wrecks, anti-Semites,
eaters of dead flies and carpet carriers.

Distillation becomes an obsession.
The beauty of its apparatus, counting
the gathering drips, fractional, his chemistry
days at Oxford, the First – abandoned for what?

1. A TURNIP TAKES THE VEIL

*"Now as I traverse this land, which
hath made a fearful wreck of itself,
I shall chronicle such tales as befit
a buffoons' buffet – sandwiches of shit."*

(Dave Turnip, "Pindaric Odes to Diversity")

Like any old Victorian madman,
Turnip controls time, watching the sea widen
between boat and shore.

Eliot's nocturnal peregrinations, his wording
soothing as a bath – to roll in such water.

Reading to his father – and a blind woman,
the smoke tincture of midwinter England,
now minus faith but still with its poets.

To wear a burkha fits his smog and hatred:
why not Dave Turnip enshrouded?

Memories of his sister,
grabbed by an Arab woman
to size clothes, in 1970s' Brent Cross.

Basingstoke is perfect,
vague as a paperclip.

First a supermarket butcher, to purchase products
utterly porcine, swinish even,
snuffling on acorns
from dark woods to the slab.

For good measure, a Koran is carried.
His energy of release burning through the clothes,
"Allah Akbar, Mustava a Salami, Shashlik, Bhuna"–
cosmopolitan monoculturalism.

With little delay a squad car arrives.
A mob has gathered, defrocked,
scurf infested.

Their smells give raptures, half-memories of
hair gel in drizzle; African Lynx, Old Spice.

Turnip deracinated, recalls Sheringham, 2010 –
Islamicist swimming in her binbag.

He was eating chips, discussing integration,
provoking uproar in a pub quiz
("Who was St Kevin?"
"The Patron Saint of Pikeys").

Seeing his people beyond redemption,
meals at Harvester, their gross weight,
the landlord declining his suggestion
(a weighbridge, to avoid congestion).

But in cities,
the weight of people is
impossible to resist.

How can it exist –
a home? Surely the mob
would tear it down.

Turnip wasn't mistreated, enjoying prison:
no doubt we're safer with him inside.

2. DAVE TURNIP IN HIS OWN WORDS

A. Mea Culpa

God alone knows, I'm a non-entity.

Still, this account details how I acquired my "nom-de-guerre".

Boredom as the floodwater. Its incessant lapping, hesitating, hiding (add what you want); concatenating – a term from my chemical days – is just such a trick.

Like most of my class, educated in the free 80s, dragged through that nauseating zone where academia meets liberal privilege. Haunted by unreasonable – often cruel – resentments.

It comes from years of lies, fake empathy and non-guilty professions of guilt.

Luckily my politics aren't of the left.

B. Reification of such contortions

I attend an open-floor limbo dancing club, in Harlesden. Disguised in my retro-parker and ponytail.

Alternate Tuesdays, Polly Toynbee attempts to lower herself under the bar, jeered at and showered in lager by the very class she patronises – once appearing in her office cleaner's uniform; perhaps you recall she did an Orwell and got such a job – "seeing what it's like to live as an unskilled worker".

C. My incident (not in the Tottenham Court Road)

I arrive and park; strange crowds coagulate, waiting.

Blind ravens before an execution.
An enormous burger woman is kicking her child, using alternate feet.
Mobile tucked between slabs of chin;
removed once, to snap then send images.

Once I would have reflected.

Running at me, down the street,
an emaciated and naked figure,
genitals painted phosphorescent green.

People step aside as my arms are pinioned then lower garments removed.
From the drive of a pebble-dashed bungalow, a large cannon is rolled forward.

His twiglet fingers grasp my shoulders.
I am invited to kiss the gunner's daughter.

D. The effect

My first evening of lone drinking was a disaster. Every pub showed a looped clip of my aforementioned ordeal.

Close-ups of my grimacing face drew howls of execration and massed conga dancing.

E. The aftermath

I dined in Pizza Express. That enormous bitch was there, douching with garlic butter and force-feeding dough balls to her bruised son.

Social mobility.

F. The plea bargain

I am bitterly aware how unexceptional was my experience and how pointless and unreadable is this account. In mitigation, I can honestly say how lacking in pungency and bite has been anything else I could recount.

G. Substance

How could they.

Drugs mean different things.
A quick foray into rich territory,
Sunday supplement exotica.

Or grimy curtains on flickering rooms:

A lost little boy on the veranda,
Jessie telling him to play peek-a-boo,
knowing now there's not a thing he can do.

Paul Sutton

H. I am one

The hard thing not saying but meaning it,
the move to this county a disaster –
a deep-time quiet of endless woods, hiding
crime after crime after crime after crime.

Tales and parables told by evacuated villagers,
every night before the firewood goes;
scars, prison tattoos, bullets never removed so
skin forms over a trace-work of escape.

A shotgun and birds scattering.
Snow-fog linking the golf course,
redbrick house, coast road.

One whole evening by a rattling door.
Every arrival meeting me face on,
elbowing through, collapsing at the bar.

A database of all the occupants:
those who left the city when I did,
children adopted after their parents disappeared,
a few locals who feign ignorance or incomprehension.

My nightly reading becomes a weekly writing,
chronicling: nature notes and casual conversation.

So skilled now, no counting needed; coding by syllable.

Long ago, my failed dissertation,
on the dystopian perfection of
And Then There Were None.

Attracting some unnamed in a Ministry,
looking for a failure seeking revenge,
(see Banquo's killers).

I know it always seems grim,
but there's perfection in emptiness –
a featureless coast where nothing happens.

I. All roads filled

Emptied the house, barely looking at things;
car waiting, loyal and uncomplaining.

On the Norfolk coast, views to the Arctic,
I check my fingers and toes for safety.

Writers move here and sit in empty pubs.
I watch one count his unsold collections,

piling copies under different tables,
inscribing them to random phonebook names.

The secret? To avoid exclamation –
self-deprecation which no one believes.

J. TripAdvisor my preferred reading

Wherever the arrow falls, a body is found.
The constant nudging of his elbows
forcing my grandfather to emigrate.

Arriving by sea, regretting leaving,
walking the elevated roads, eventually
finding a motel called "Vermins".

The Nanford Hotel for dying rodents,
occupants flying kites made from
failed restaurant table cloths.

K. Upriver until the water runs clean

To be there inside, when the door is kicked:
violent layers of ubberchavs, gestating
in the cracks between equality and extermination.

How right was Kurtz, striking like summer lightning –
Sickert's figures chasing each other over cliffs,
emerging into gallery spaces and repetitions of white.

Wherever you run to I will find,
be it oblivion or unlit retail units.

L. Unusual cloud formations

Limited in subject? Remember they know
more than entire families, even estates,
in such towns where bodies are barely
literate before demanding.

Droll to say it, but love for your
fellow man is a nonsense here, only
idiots and – what's worse – their
advisors – can afford such bilge.

It's enough to avoid them when driving –
I swear I almost always swerve, when
entering the local schools or estates:
Foot down? Only just the once or twice.

M. Revenant passes unseen

In frequent returns here, the territory seems
unchanged, a repeat gesture which fails.

However absurd the forms are, some take
delight in their filling, judging, delivering.

I barely conceal my contempt, ask if she
knows how much harm her sort has done.

Her smile invites violence, the need for
expletives, a certainty of any death soon.

N. Observation by morons

If I want to find things out,
I wait expect ask decide.

Paul Sutton

Dancing in the corridors,
the ageing hen-party hopefuls.

I put up my body for attacking;
odd, given my nervous past.

Without wishing to sound ungrateful,
they burnt me alive – without fail.

O. Clearing

Emptying her house, starting in calmness,
cis-trans flipping into frenzy.

The early calculators – a Sinclair
programmable, random flashes.

It barely worked, the manual still
my delight, its optimism and precision.

Now I live in hotels. They call me
"tip-toer". Waiting until the 2am all-quiet.

So many corridors, in uniformity my
comfort; static on the stair-rail.

By breakfast I've finished.

P. Stay off the moors

Dropping like curtains in Bath,
seen through the wet walk from
the station. Just like that boy
in Roald Dahl's taxidermist story.
I like being lonely in pubs,
providing there's an open fire –
and people at the bar to hide me.
I've stayed in a few – even walked
through fog, miles from any road,
barely drunk – or only on whisky,
which causes glowing not stumbling.
Fans of horror stories know the details,
be it dogs or seagulls or some American
whose presence causes silence and then,
a missed dart. What I didn't know was
how I'd miss it all – the cold walk to
the toilets, the overlong menu;
I checked in and fainted, was carried
upstairs and thrown out the window –
into the millstream and out to sea.

Q. Thrown away

Their best track, purest pride in rejection,
head down and unapologetic. To hear a mother
sing to her child – the purest sound – even
if you leave now, it will follow you everywhere.

"Our ships will stay for just a moment" and
in going take the bits no one noticed,
edges half-seen – not the word "liminal" –
too poetic, when the image is all.

I stood and watched as they went,
empty but fulfilled, certain of
my certainty, felt the gales changing
and the flames were welcome.

R. Haunting of the second-homer

Washed up onshore. I lay there for a week,
then removed the seaweed and bladderwrack.
Delightful, criss-crossing the town unseen,
sitting in converted chandlers, sipping white wine,
stealing from tables, pushing children over seawalls.
The place I stayed was an old lighthouse,
glowering over the salt marsh. I launched
from the top-rail, landing in mud suction:
hysterical owner screaming as she woke.
The woman wrote a novel, based on my
bullshit messages: copperplate letters
from a wronged housemaid, deflowered,
abandoned – drowning herself in black mud.
I enjoyed the book-launch, hurling pigshit
at the pony-tailed publisher. The granary
location went up like a vodka factory.
Oh Norfolk, you need the arts industry,
my hate destroyed this opportunity.

S. Mansion block, Maida Vale

In service, 1.3 million, under street grids;
I never lived in basement flats – flooding,
ghosts, silver for polishing, original features:
concierge's room (he arranged the burglaries).

About an hour of silence, between two and four.
The place was ugly but comforting. German bombs
bounced off, but not suited for drops in status –
last time driving past, it was gone.

T. Threatened

I don't think
things can be
pretty or ugly.
All that you can say
is if your existence
is not threatened
in any way.

My first track, Southampton Gaumont,
a stark rejoinder to the lumpen,
a class issue, as always –
perhaps none of the left wanted this.

I was scarred by all those early journeys,
the New Towns, to slums, Caledonian Road;
even then the cold light was different,
seats blue striped, shaded, long nationalised.

Consumption levelled it all.
The odd head poked up, to
be knocked down like a nail;
once through my foot,
a central pain, that
collapsed to a swivel.

3. ANOTHER WRETCHED DAY IN BLIGHTY (AN INTERLUDE, IN WHICH YOUR AUTHOR OFFERS HIS PIQUANT OBSERVATIONS)

Vindictive rain soaks the bovine as they queue – for what? It scarcely matters; perhaps just to pass the time.

Armitage and Duffy arrive in a cavalcade, spraying freezing water over the huddled masses, who raise a feeble cheer as Armitage flashes his Hawaiian shirt.

Immediately, a phalanx of local poets rush forward, slim volumes offered up for the great man to touch, like scrofula lepers with suppurating sores.

The crowd are desperate now. One mendicant, stained a livid yellow – as of curried vomit – literally hurls himself at Armitage's feet.

He steps over him, with the unhurried delicacy of an Ancien Régime French aristocrat.

Bring forth the guillotine.

Yes, I find this bleakness inspiring but, step back and one feels; who the fuck could live here?

I've also seen aged crones howling at the lowering sky, tearing their flesh and begging the bin men to drag them off.

Locals wheeling their failed lives in concentric circles around a central reservation of lard.

Babies in prams eating Greggs' sausage rolls, glimpsed through a mist of fag smoke.

Impossible to comment on.

**4. THE TURNIP'S RETURN
(narrated by Sutton)**

A. Prologue by an icy stream

Unrecognized now,
anyway all mostly dead
(the last friends from his days of twitching).

In the wind-whacked days of January,
a stranger to old Norfolk, arriving
by taxi from central London, trudging
the last few miles through quagmire and goose shit.

Settling for this.
A single chair by the fire –
his need for discomfort when writing.

Dave Turnip is falling from all our sight,
rebooting old laptops for long-lost files:
accounts of bird arrivals and car deaths,
drownings in the rivers east of Wisbech.

To swim daily in
a mushy-pea coloured ditch;
routines key to his resurrection.

B. Intimate witness

When I first met him, there wasn't a hint who he was – or thought he was.
So many of them anyway, drinking alone (The Chequers, Wimbotsham),
each at their own table, no conversation, just the minimum to order food
and drink.

I'm originally a country yokel and resent these middle class second-homers – although this rather flat account makes my register sound higher than usual.

But your writer can't be bothered to be authentic. So my voice won't sound real, which is useful.

Forget anything in dialect – or chav speak, text talk, Caribbean drugs lingo – that's all bollocks too.

And forget poetry. You'd sooner read a planning application.

I think these poor bastards saw the county sign and bought the first empty barn.

Ditches here run straight as my dreary thoughts.

I'd never seen anyone so thin, nor with so curved a spine; almost like a cartoon walking stick.

He showed me some of his poetry. I couldn't read it – I mean literally; might as well have been in Albanian.

When he said he was called Dave Turnip, I though it was apt – remembering some quote about the counties east of London.

To be honest, he gave me the shakes, with his photographing of rivers in which local people drowned.

He used an eel fisherman – the bloke's been on *Countryfile*, a real artisan, dying breed, up at dawn, near-empty nets, sole survivor – now the east Europeans have eaten all the fish.

C. All the way to The Wash

The thing about Turnip is what he knows.
For instance, the methods pick-pockets use,
from friendship with a midget Brazilian –
take: two grand a day at Oxford Circus.

Which king died from a surfeit of lampreys?
The first question in each Monday's pub quiz,
he still shouts the answer with real pleasure.
How to tell genuine from fake ruby.

Expert on house breaking. Incredible
how he learnt it. A Norfolk holiday
and he started an Agatha Christie,
mildewed copy found in the old cottage.

Stuck in Thetford, mind-attacking traffic.
Who did it; vicar or "drug-fiend" sister?
He sees the book left by a brick fireplace...
Back – calm, night entry, someone sleeping. His.

And then it becomes an addiction, like
we all have nowadays. The clean purpose,
transgressive, every hatred of his class.
He was never caught, what he took worthless.

D. Interested bystander

Turnip's father was a food technologist, who rose to prominence in the world of biscuits. His Reading factory was a world centre for this obscurantist – but lucrative – trade. Many was the tirade he gave on Lincolns, Dairy Milks, Orange Puffs, Abbey Crunches, Ginger Nuts, Garibaldis.

He despised the easy charm of Jaffa Cakes and Bourbons.

When you hear of DT's childhood, it's not surprising he turned out like this.

Oh, I'm aware "this" still reads flat.

But forget artifice.

In fact, art.

What we have here is sky, pylons, the lorry swish in rain or sun. Little Chefs.

Forget the farmers' markets too. That's for the West Country, with its fake Celts and piri-piri refugees.

Emneth Hungate!

I took him to see Tony Martin's house – a near shrine for the vicious, the flatlanders, the people brought up with rain on their face.

People like me, who clutch carrier bags and can't push a pram without chipping your heels.

He fell to his knees, sobbing and clutching the sodden earth, smearing it over his face and chest.

We looked over the battered ruin – Martin long since flown, to some parched ochre hideout on the Costa.

Back in Wimbotsham, I'd never seen him happier.

Let me explain:

His project – with the eel fisherman – was producing! Somehow he'd persuaded a Cromer poetry publisher to takes his grotesque photo-journal; *Fenland Locations for a-Drownin'*.

Misty, crepuscular shots, alongside his tender and spare lyrics. As a sensitive man, he was disguising the actual names – which reduced the risk of lynching, by:

July Stevens (mother of "The Blob", Great Ouse).
Tim Clanchey (brother of "The Floater", The Black Sluice).
Anabelle Richards (sister of "Ophelia", Dead Rats' Cutting).
Cecelia Wake (daughter of "Weir-blocker", North Brink).
Varlid Aronsonvikiliski (father of "Good riddance, Drug Boy", Sutton's Culvert).

So, where do I fit in? A gofer, his bob-a-job bit of local colour, with contacts – or enemies – through this benighted land.

Turnip has no idea I'm a poet.

E. Photo-shoot

Any colder and your nose would drop off.
The river mist here falls from a zinc sky,
suddenly one's lost in the sound of drips.
Turnip launches into khaki water.

He insists on a fish's eye view as
the last thing the bedraggled local saw –
often an upshot through closing water.
If that's horrible, try reading the verse:

"Farewell to my anorexia, thin
as a whippet running over fenland.
Dear father, I can't live any longer
on a diet of two baked beans a day.

I remember my first sight of the deer,
our last holiday ever with mother.
It approached the patio doors and tapped;
so, welcome me now, maternal water."

F. Some context

Frankly (one of my favourite words) who needs this stuff?

Not even a buyer's market. No market, just a long view into an empty sky.

Yet DT recounts grizzly tales of the dynastic bloodshed swirling through the "poetry world".

He's convinced his tasteless parodying of lyrical beauty may "tap into a wider audience".

As evidence, he posits a disgraceful incident at Heaney's most recent benediction to the English plebs, in London's Bloomsbury Theatre (the very name makes you yearn for violence).

A Bolano type stunt:

Heaney is back in the bogs, some or other peat-preserved corpse dug up then washed down with holy water.

An enormous fart rings the air. The sound is like a sail ripping. It must last at least twenty seconds, with no drop in intensity – if anything, gathering into a juddering climax.

Heaney attempts humour: "Someone's been on the marsh cabbages – how I remember them from convent school."

But the spell is broken.

An outraged "Irish" American dropkicks DT unconscious.

But not before the sound of clapping softens his fall.

Subsequent blacklisting was inevitable.

Every poetry outlet in the country hauled up the drawbridge.

Even the "Back Room Poets" refused him floor space.

The Fens became his only option.

G. Why I write

So many times I sat and stared at walls.
Hearing the micro-sounds flaking away
the one thing I ever had that was mine.
And time is caught now in my case of words.

I send this stuff off anonymously,
most assume I'm playing it all for laughs –
although they could never raise one themselves.

Hand in hand walking to the coast one night.
DT and I shout remembered poems
into the thankfully unconcerned sky:

5. THE SORRY HISTORY OF FAST FOOD
(co-authored, Sutton/Turnip)

A. Political Property

I.

Of course haunting is true,
wherever it comes from. Perhaps
one-in-ten homes are memory traps.

I mean those gravel-rendered
semis of the London suburbs.
Desolation in the heat or rain.

Almost an old man, in the sickly
quiet of hedges behind plane trees.
I was followed back once.

Nothing to worry you now.
A man of string, fingers
clutching dead mice.

II.

When I watch property programmes,
I'm astounded that places I shuddered
from as slums, now sell for millions.
Actually, the worst glowered down on
Euston Road, where Capital Radio went.
I saw it from the old hospital, wondering
'Who lives behind those perforated curtains?'
and beneath the archway was a grim ravine.

Paul Sutton

The areas around old stations did it best.
That's why regeneration of King's Cross,
or even worse Paddington, was such a loss.
Remember those Italian cafes, which served
spaghetti to toothy war brides and cascading
knickerbocker glories to girls clutching dolls?
We knew the coffee was Thames mud and
loved it all the more for being so bad.

There's no doubt we were filthier then
and our teeth lurked like mustard gas.
What's really changed though are smells;
shops then – cardboard and the saturated
expected aroma of an old man's crotch.
London was wonderful in soot and dust,
even the rain smelt like bomb damage and
stations of cigarettes which can't be captured.

On warm evenings, I go back to school for a
production. That vast sun through plate glass,
in a summer of total heat. Guessing there was
any government, happy or just funding it, in
the sure assumption of Garden City utopia –
they felt class had finished –
it hadn't of course, although
for children it could be true.

III.

A drowned baby, bare
feet stand on its back.

Men in top-hats decapitated, masked
activists kick their heads into the sea.

(Stop any agreement, daemon
with a frozen logic of virtue.)

Just nothing for defying ochlocracy:
a mass rally screaming its sanctimony.

Projected into my home and body.
I can't complain though.

The sun still shines, so the garden
shows pure green in warming blue.

I can masturbate at leisure
now frozen food is available.

Not from the sky, but some movement
in the pine trees has me unconcerned.

B. A History of Heatwaves

It started in 1976. I never realised
why English people feared the sun.

That green of suffocation. Cycling
a wooded lane, shadows glimpsed
in a river. Seen too near, as ghosts.

Intoxication, of elderflower and wild,
sharp roots. Anyone can find the centre
in hidden woods and no one goes there.

C. My Boy Jack

I.

My first visit to the Jack the Ripper
conference; in a shivery suit, shiny
yet pasty faced. I could have been
some pallid clerk, a spring-heeled
escapee from the Abyss.

How naïve not to realise
that others do the same;
proposing an ancestor
as the latest suspect.

My great-uncle's disgraceful papers.

Some motorway service station.

(Impossible not to love them,
their invocation of oblivion;
a linear fast-food heaven.

My record was five hours
spent eating and defecating.)

Underneath an abandoned mop.
His old journal, sealed in pig fat.

II.

(from *The Journal of Mutatis Mutandis*)

Fuck me, I'm tired.

Spent.

Like a ginger beer bottle, exploding at some daft street fair.

Now my sons, look at that photograph of me in whiskers.

My ramrod cock hidden.

An iron stare.

Clearly a cunt – and you only know the half.

Too easy avoiding the 'rozzers'.

I used an electric moped – though scarcely invented then – working as a pizza delivery boy.

No one suspected a thing!

My blood-spotted uniform
taken as some new topping.

The area was gentrifying
from days of plague dogs
and leper chips.

Opportunities overflowing.

Why these immigrants –
to chronicle the rain?

I now explain my actions in terms of diversification.
Providing a safe environment, where creative types
can network and rediscover squalor – at a distance.

III.

"Preposterous.

Monstrous.

Tedious."

(A letter, from the Psychogeographic Poets.)

"Sinclairian rehash! Another rip-off
 bike-seat sniffer on Saucy Jack riff."

Many poets moved to Spitalfields.
Drinking wheatbeer where his
'Unfortunates' slugged gin.

Leylines, ranting tracts,
recycled toe rags from
forgotten antiquarians.

Ridiculous – our true country
is pure retail park, B & Q.

D. My work on TripAdvisor

God knows why Wetherspoons is sneered at.
It's the equivalent of a Victorian chophouse.

More genuine than identikit gastropubs –
infinite goatees, gorging on brick or slate.

Let's admit to it, the English
have always scoffed anything.

I can trace my history
through such disasters.

Did you try Elizabethan
"offal and hoof quickbits"
on the dizzy South Bank?

Or the "chipped potatoes"
on Whitechapel Road?

Boiled cabbage greens,
the grease on the cobbles,
a trudge to the next house.

It wasn't much.

Paul Sutton

E. Street Chicken

I am now convinced that my old Cambridge tutor – Maxwell Otto Cornelius – was Jack the Ripper.

Item 1:

A sperm-stained copy of Newton's *Principia*.

Purloined from Trinity library,
endpapers removed,
passages redacted.

Repetitive marginalia:

"Exterminate the brutes!"

Item 2:

A complex amalgam of hieroglyphs, pentagrams, ostrich feathers and fast-food napkins.

Specific links to Poussin's *A Dance to the Music of Time* – erroneous Latin motto, wrongly attributed to George Formby.

Item 3:

Space prohibits a fuller explanation of my methods.

Viz:

DNA testing on seagull carcass remains, with cross-referencing to filial genomes and mutant Subway chicken wraps, matches 92% hypochondriacal material to a towering Latvian lady, now working in Nando's.

Cornelius obsessed with her – proposing marriage.

Rejection spawning incipient misogyny and insanity.

A fast train to King's Cross – then underground to Aldgate East.

I myself espied him
in a Brick Lane tandoori;
ruddy stains on fingers and wrists.

Engaged in diversionary assault on poppadoms –
numerous lurid dips – one of bright carnelian red.

Perfect trace element match re.
ink in *Dear Boss* letter.

F. Human once

Where is the pity
in any of this?

Easy to objectify,
in black and white.

No access to their
memories: smiles
as a child of joy;
dad thowing them
in the air and then
held secure.

G. Jupiter

Holst's giddy joy,
a pride, history and triumph –
you to play it, again, again,
in green English fields –
assurance, love, trust.

It's now I need to write of it;
in some tone to match
old feelings with words.

Cut away this soggy and anxious fog.
Somewhere over the western waves
return to shade, a sapphire light,
and melodies by river meadows,
not caring when lost.

Why any shame in writing about this?
It's only a sound,
pure cadence;
just words.

H. Rituals around the dead

They show their videos:

Last meals; threats; landscapes; words.
Broadcast into loved ones' dreams –
a jolt, then we long for the repeat.

On a coast of ruined industry.

People who never see
far-distant mountains
or feel pine-cool air.

The bodies carried into parched fields.

To long mangled and dead trees,
then dissected in intricate ways –
from texts by 19th-century maniacs.

It doesn't matter now; they're 'passed'.

But the food eaten greedily
at these Saturnalian rituals?
It is of the worst kind.

The heat is all I recall.

In suffocating
nights under a
flickering sky.

Wet of sweat-
tangled dreams,
creeper bound.

Tarred, fly-devoured.
Driven near dawn into
yellow-throned swamp.

I. The Room

There is a room where everyone goes.
I don't mean death, or anything close.

The body drags around a mind,
then one day leaves it behind.

Long lost as animals;
believing in thoughts,

worshipping identical
sensations. Radiation

just whacks us forever.
And only pity matters.

EPILOGUE (ON UVB-76)

All these noise in my head,
voices and buzzing. Giving

up a country for fancy bread.
On shortwave radio, I hear war

chatter. I move into a bunker and
imagine pines, sand dunes, the stars.

When can we two be together, my friend?
On this frequency forever – without end.

www.ingramcontent.com/pod-product-compliance
Lightning Source LLC
Chambersburg PA
CBHW051703040426
42446CB00009B/1274